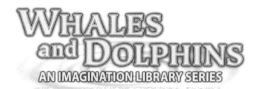

BLUE WHALES

by Victor Gentle and Janet Perry

Gareth Stevens Publishing
A WORLD ALMANAC EDUCATION GROUP COMPANY

Please visit our web site at: www.garethstevens.com
For a free color catalog describing Gareth Stevens' list of high-quality books and
multimedia programs, call 1-800-542-2595 (USA) or 1-800-461-9120 (Canada).
Gareth Stevens Publishing's Fax: (414) 332-3567.

Library of Congress Cataloging-in-Publication Data

Gentle, Victor.
    Blue whales / by Victor Gentle and Janet Perry.
        p. cm. — (Whales and dolphins: an imagination library series)
    Includes bibliographical references and index.
    ISBN 0-8368-2880-1 (lib. bdg.)
        1. Blue whale—Juvenile literature. [1. Blue whale. 2. Whales.]
    I. Perry, Janet, 1960- II. Title.
    QL737.C424G458   2001
    599.5'248—dc21   2001020011

First published in 2001 by
Gareth Stevens Publishing
A World Almanac Education Group Company
330 West Olive Street, Suite 100
Milwaukee, WI 53212 USA

Text: Victor Gentle and Janet Perry
Art direction: Karen Knutson
Page layout: Victor Gentle, Janet Perry, Joel Bucaro, and Tammy Gruenewald
Cover design: Joel Bucaro
Series editor: Catherine Gardner
Picture Researcher: Diane Laska-Swanke

Photo credits: Cover, pp. 9 (main), 15 © Doc White/Seapics.com; p. 5 (main) © Phillip
Colla/Seapics.com; pp. 5 (inset), 17 © Hiroya Minakuchi/Seapics.com; p. 7 (main)
© Mark Conlin/Seapics.com; p. 7 (inset) © Doug Perrine/Seapics.com; p. 9 (inset)
© Ingrid Visser/Seapics.com; p. 11 © Bob Cranston/Seapics.com; p. 13 © François Gohier;
p. 19 © Marilyn Kazmers/Seapics.com; p. 21 © Mike Johnson/Seapics.com; p. 22
Joel Bucaro/© Gareth Stevens, Inc., 2001

Printed in the United States of America

1 2 3 4 5 6 7 8 9 05 04 03 02 01

Front cover: Blue whales have 55 to 80 throat
pleats that expand so they can fill their mouths
with millions of krill and gallons of water!

TABLE OF CONTENTS

Words that appear in the glossary are printed in **boldface** type the first time they occur in the text.

THE BLUES, BLOWING LOUD

When a blue whale blows, it makes a noise loud enough to be heard a mile away — over howling winds, crashing waves, and roaring boat engines. When a blue whale rumbles underwater, other whales can hear the sound for thousands of miles.

When a blue whale dives, its back seems to go on and on. You could easily read this page, draw a picture, or finish your math homework while you waited for it to plunge into the sea and wave bye-bye with **flukes** as wide as a bus is long.

While a blue whale feeds, it gulps tons of tiny animals and many swimming pools full of water — in every mouthful! Blue whales are BIG.

Main photo: This blue whale's **blowholes** look like a gigantic upside-down nose on the top of its head. Inset: You could fit inside one of the nostrils!

RECORD BLUES

The blue whale is the biggest animal that has ever lived on Earth. Bigger than dinosaurs? Yes! Scientists guess that the biggest dinosaur was about 130 feet (39.6 meters) long and weighed about 220,000 pounds (99,800 kilograms).

Norwegian whalers claim to have caught a blue whale that weighed almost twice as much. They say it was 100 feet (30.5 m) long and weighed about 400,000 pounds (181,500 kg), which is heavier than 30 tyrannosaurus rexes.

Most blue whales alive today are about 80 feet (24.4 m) long and weigh about 320,000 pounds (145,150 kg).

Main photo: Blue whales are so big and fast that we use skeletons to estimate their size. Inset: A man easily fits inside a blue whale's rib bones.

BIG APPETITE!

If you were as big as 30 Indian elephants, how much food would you need? *A lot!* A fully grown blue whale eats during about eight months of the year. For four of those months it gobbles up about 8,000 pounds (3,600 kg) of food a day. In human food, that would be 14,000 carrots, 1,200 bowls of thick soup, and 4 whole cows (bones and all) every day for four whole months!

Blue whales are the biggest animals on Earth, and yet, they eat the smallest animals in the sea — **krill**. Krill are tiny, shrimplike **crustaceans** that are about as long as a person's thumb — 1 to 2.5 inches (2.5 to 6.4 centimeters). A bucket of krill-filled ocean water would hold over 100 of the little beasties.

Main photo: *Balaenoptera musculus* is the blue whale's scientific name. Inset: Some krill are only about an inch long. In Norwegian, *"kril"* means "whale food."

WAVES OF PINK AND BLUES

Blue whales do not eat krill one by one. They could never eat enough that way. Instead, these whales **lunge-feed**. (Don't try this at home!) A blue whale dives and then swims up through its food. With its mouth open w–i–d–e, it scoops in water filled with pink waves of krill. Its throat pleats expand like a gigantic accordion, all the way to its belly button.

Then, the whale rolls onto its side to slop out some of the water. Its massive tongue squeezes the water through plates of **baleen** that hang from the roof of its mouth. These are about 3 feet (1 m) long and are made of the same stuff as fingernails. A blue whale sucks about 40 million krill from its baleen in a day.

This blue whale lunge-feeds at the surface of the water. A small boat could fit inside its wide-open mouth. Gulls wisely flee when blues feed.

BABY BLUES

Each year, blue whales **migrate** from feeding grounds to breeding grounds, where their **calves** are born. In one day, a blue whale calf drinks 50 gallons (190 liters) of its mother's milk and gains 200 pounds (91 kg). In seven months, it grows almost as big as an adult blue whale. At a year old, the calf must be able to take care of itself.

After feeding their calves mama blues are *starving!* It is a good thing they can swim fast back to their feeding grounds, where **shoals** of krill drift in columns as tall and as wide as a 30-story building. Blue whales swim all day at about 14 miles per hour (22 kilometers per hour). Olympic champions can swim only about 2 mph (3 km/h) for just minutes at a time.

This baby blue is **breaching**. There are many reasons why blues leap free of the water like this. They may be playing, building up speed, or just looking around.

BLUE STREAK

How can an animal as long as seven or eight jeeps and as heavy as a herd of cattle swim faster than a champion human swimmer?

A blue whale's long, slender body is shaped like a speedboat. Its head has a ridge from the blowholes to the snout that helps the whale slice through the water. Because most of its muscle is in its tail, a blue whale surges through the water with each stroke of its powerful flukes.

A blue whale also has a lot of blubber, or fat. Blubber keeps the blue whale warm and helps it store food. It helps the whale float, too. Otherwise, the whale would have to use some of its precious energy to keep from sinking.

Blue whales' tails are like huge, powerful engines. At top speed, blues race 30 mph (48 km/h), sometimes riding another blue's wave.

GETTING THE BLUES

At one time, being speedy and huge kept blue whales safe from whalers. After they were harpooned, blues swam so fast that they ripped apart the small whaling ships of long ago. If they died, blues were too heavy to carry to shore.

In 1864, however, Norwegian Sven Foyn invented the exploding harpoon, which killed a blue whale instantly. Then came the modern factory ships. They were big enough and fast enough to catch a blue and pull it on board for processing.

In 1864, there were hundreds of thousands of blue whales. By 1964, there were fewer than 10,000. In 100 years, one blue whale's lifetime, blues were almost **extinct**.

Scientists think that blue whales should live to be 100 years old. Between 1864 and 1964, the oldest and largest blue whales in the world were killed.

LEARNING ABOUT THE BLUES

In 1966, the International Whaling Commission declared that blue whales must be protected from whalers. Since then, whale watchers have learned that blue whales are doing their best to survive against other dangers.

Females used to start breeding at ten years old, but now they start at seven. More blue whales now **calve** once every two years, instead of once every three years. Still, their numbers are not growing.

In some areas, there are not enough blue whales to mate with each other. Instead, they seem to be mating with other **species**, such as fin whales. Unfortunately, the **hybrid** offspring of blue whales with other species are not protected from whalers.

Is this a good-bye flick of the fluke from the last of the blues — or can we help them save their beautiful blue and gray spotted skins?

DEATH OF THE BLUES?

The idea that blue whales and other whales might create whole new species is exciting. Yet, it would be sad if pure blue whales died out completely. We have just begun to know them.

Sixty years ago, we finally heard blue whales. At 180 decibels, they are as loud as an airplane, but the sound is so low that you can only feel it. As blues call to and answer each other across wide seas, we just feel thunder in our chests, around our hearts.

Long ago, the oceans rumbled with the sounds of hundreds of thousands of blue whales! Older blue whales must feel that the oceans are terribly quiet now. Perhaps, someday, the oceans, and our hearts, will once again swell with the sounds of big blues.

What "instrument" do blues play — their baleen, their skull, their ribs, or their lungs? If we cannot study living blues, we might never find out.

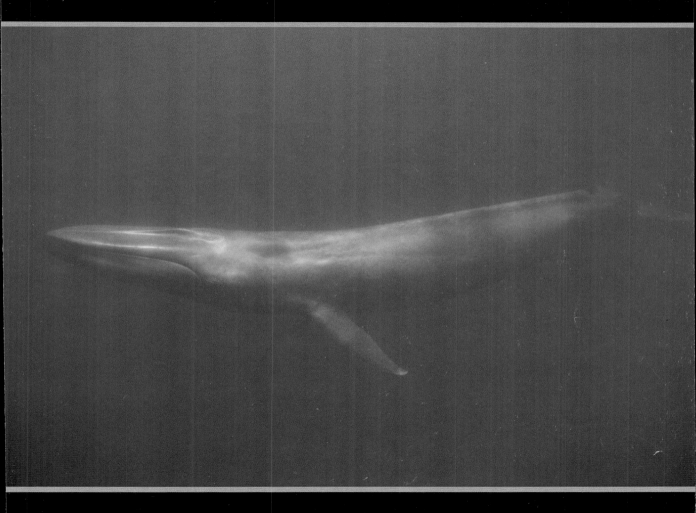

MORE TO READ AND VIEW

Books (Nonfiction)   *Blue Whale.* Rod Theodorou (Heinemann Library)
Whales and Dolphins (series). Victor Gentle and Janet Perry
   (Gareth Stevens)
Whales, Dolphins, and Porpoises. Mark Carwardine (Dorling Kindersley)
Whales: Killer Whales, Blue Whales, and More. Deborah Hodge
   (KidsCan Press)

Books (Fiction)   *Amigo, the Friendly Gray Whale.* [includes songs and a CD] A. Kay Lay
   (Waterborne Press)
Big Blue Whale. Nicola Davies (Candlewick Press)
The Whale's Song. Dyan Sheldon (Dial Books)
The Wild Whale Watch. Eva Moore (Scholastic)

Videos (Nonfiction)   *The Great Whales.* (National Geographic)
Whale Rescue. Wildlife Tales (series). (ABC)

BLUE WHALE QUICK FACTS

Average weight of adults
About 320,000 pounds (145,000 kg)

Average length of adults
Females: up to 110 feet (33.6 m)
Males: largest found was 88 feet (26.8 m)

Number of baleen
540 to 790 baleen plates, up to
39 inches (1 m) long

Length of life
Up to 100 years

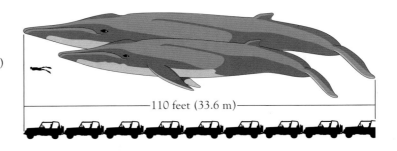

110 feet (33.6 m)

Special features
The largest blue whale's heart weighs about 1,000 pounds (450 kg) and circulates 14,000 pounds (6,400 kg) of blood through its body. An adult human being could crawl through the blue whale's largest blood vessel. Its tongue is about the same weight as its heart. Its flippers are about 8 feet (2.4 m) long. Its flukes are about 25 feet (7.6 m) wide from tip to tip.

WEB SITES

If you have your own computer and Internet access, great! If not, most libraries have Internet access. The Internet changes every day, and web sites come and go. We believe the following sites are likely to last and give the best, most appropriate links for readers to find out more about the oceans, whales, and other sea life.

To get started, enter the word "museums" in a general search engine. See if you can find a museum web page that has exhibits on ocean mammals and oceanography. If any of these museums are close to home, you can visit them in person!

www.yahooligans.com
This is a huge search engine and a great research tool for anything you might want to know. For information on whales, click on Animals under the Science & Nature heading. From the Animals page, you can hear or see whales and dolphins by clicking on Animal Sounds or Animal Pictures.

Or you may want to plug some words into the search engine to see what Yahooligans can find for you. Some words related to blue whales are *baleen*, *ancient whales*, *factory whaling ships*, and *krill*.

whale.wheelock.edu
The *WhaleNet* is packed full of the latest whale research information. Some is way cool! Click on the Students and then the WhaleNet Index button to find more buttons and links

that will help you find whale videos, hear echolocation, or ask a whale expert a question.

www.enchantedlearning.com/
Go to Zoom School and click on Whale Activities and Whale Dictionary for games, information sheets, and great links for many species of whales.

library.thinkquest.org/2946/main.htm
At this site, you'll find sounds of many types of whales and more whale information.

www.yoto98.noaa.gov/kids.htm
This site was created for the 1998 celebration of The Year of the Ocean. You'll find lots of buttons that lead you to games, coloring pages, and links. You can adopt a RADAR buoy that helps scientists collect information about the ocean and ocean life.

www.discovery.com/guides/animals/ under_water.html
Browse through information about many underwater creatures. Don't miss Long-Distance Calls: Voices of the Great Whales.

GLOSSARY

You can find these words on the pages listed. Reading a word in a sentence helps you understand it even better.

baleen (buh-LEEN) — plates of fingernail-like material that hang in the mouths of some whales and strain food from sea water 10, 20

blowhole (BLOH-hohl) — a hole that whales use for breathing 4, 14

breaching (BREECH-ing) — breaking free of the water, leaping over it 12

calve (KAV) (v) — to give birth to a baby whale 18

calves (KAVZ) (n) — baby whales 12

crustaceans (krus-TAY-shuns) — animals that breathe with gills and have outer skeletons that protect their bodies 8

extinct (ex-TINKT) — with no more members of that species alive 16

flukes (FLOOKS) — the two lobes forming a whale's tail 4, 14, 18

hybrid (HI-brid) — bred from two distinct species that have mated successfully 18

krill (KRIL) — tiny, shrimplike animals that form large shoals in the sea 8, 10, 12

lunge-feed (LUNJ-feed) — to feed with the mouth open wide, scooping in water and fish or krill 10

migrate (MY-grayt) — to travel to certain places at certain times of the year 12

shoals (SHOHLZ) — large groups of fish or krill swimming together 12

species (SPEE-shees) — a group of plants or animals that are alike in many ways 18, 20

INDEX